Creatures of Earth, Sea, and Sky

POEMS BY GEORGIA HEARD

DRAWINGS BY JENNIFER OWINGS DEWEY

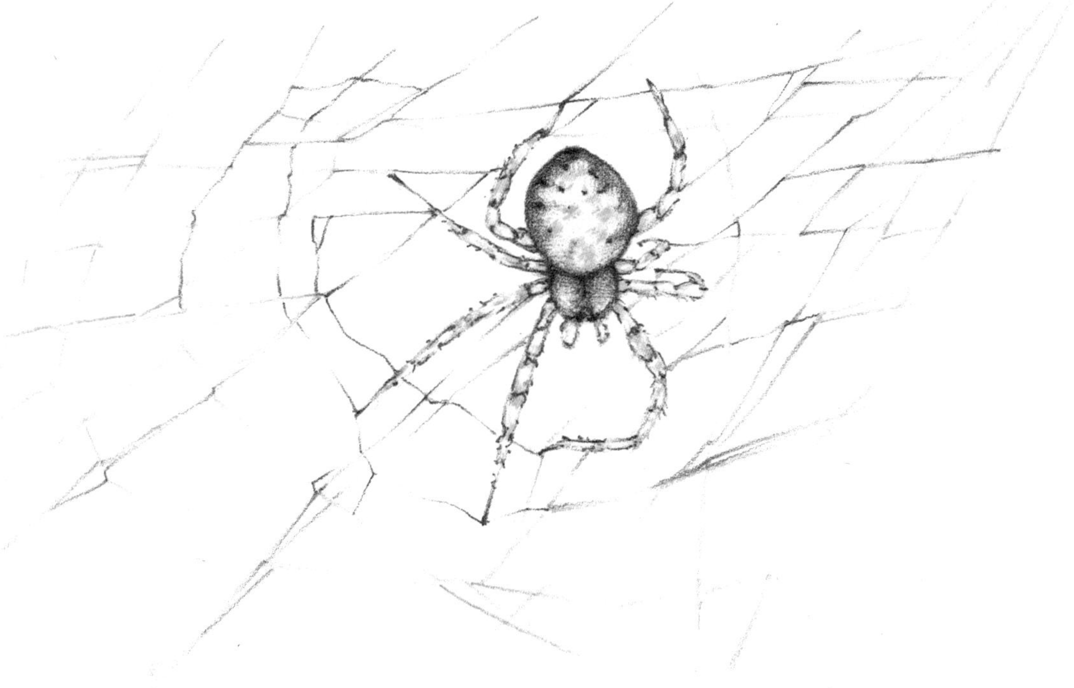

WORDSONG

Thanks to Bee, Donna, Irene, Jacqueline, Karen, Lucy, Nancy, Patty, and the East Hampton and Sag Harbor Libraries. And special thanks to Suzanne.

—G.H.

Text copyright © 1992 by Georgia Heard
Illustrations copyright © 1992 by Jennifer Owings Dewey
All rights reserved
Published by Wordsong
Boyds Mills Press, Inc.
A Highlights Company
910 Church Street
Honesdale, Pennsylvania 18431

Publisher Cataloging-in-Publication Data
Heard, Georgia.
   Creatures of earth, sea, and sky / poems by Georgia Heard ;
drawings by Jennifer Owings Dewey.
[32] p. : col. ill. ; cm.
Includes index.
Summary: Short poems for young children about wild animals.
ISBN 1-56397-013-9
1. Children's poetry—American. [1. American Poetry.]
I. Heard, Georgia.   II. Dewey, Jennifer Owings, ill.   III. Title.
811 / .54—dc20
Library of Congress Catalog Card Number: 91-65978
First edition, 1992

Book designed by Jean Krulis.
The text of this book is set in 12 point Palatino.
The drawings in this book are done in color pencil.
Distributed by St. Martin's Press
Printed in Hong Kong

10   9   8   7   6   5   4   3   2

To my mother, for Kimmy,
and for crying over *Charlotte's Web*
—G.H.

To Wheels and Sophie
—J.D.

CONTENTS

HUMMINGBIRD

Ruby-throated hummingbird
zig-
        zags
           from morning glories
to honeysuckle
        sipping
    honey
         from a straw
all day long.

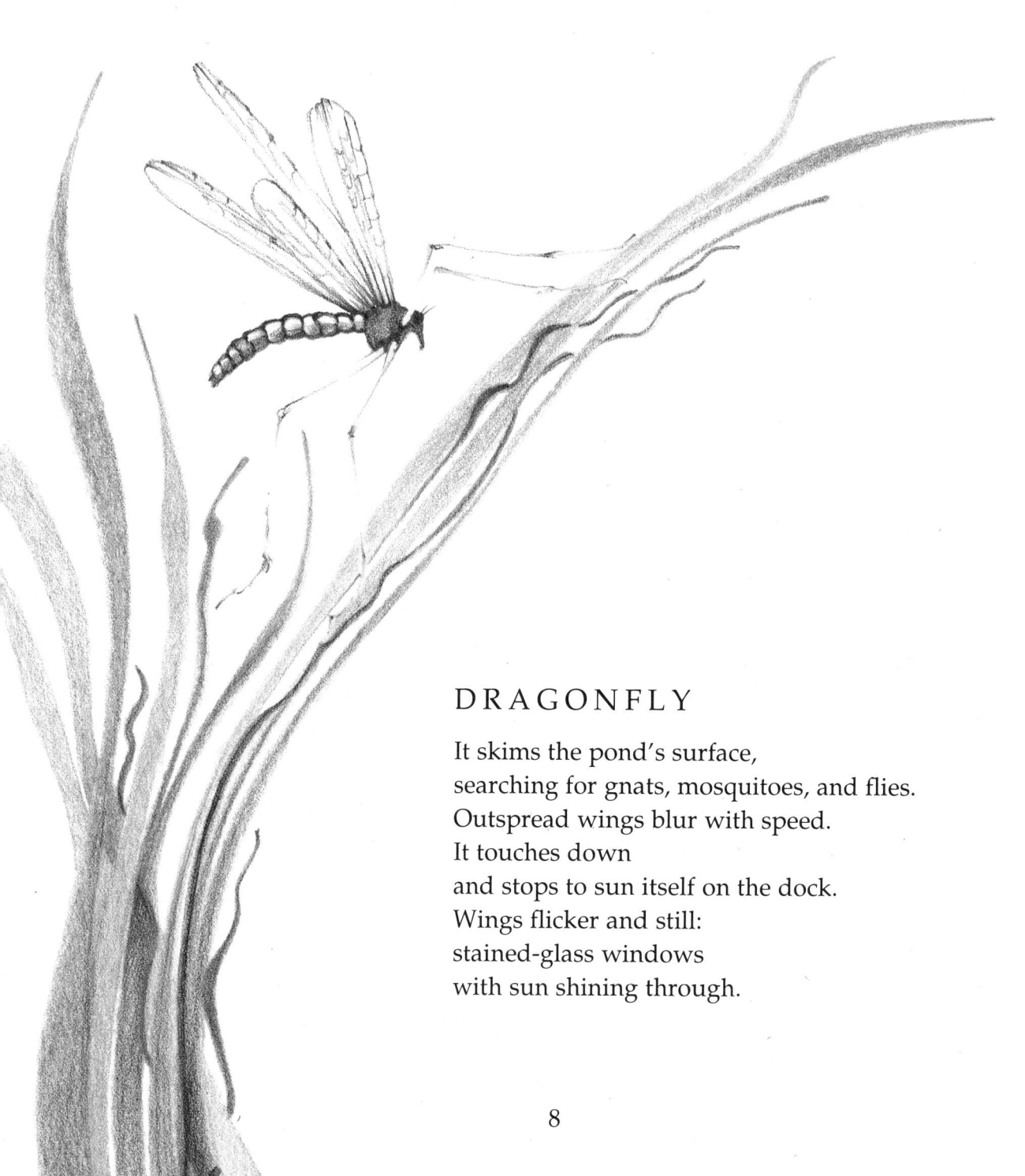

DRAGONFLY

It skims the pond's surface,
searching for gnats, mosquitoes, and flies.
Outspread wings blur with speed.
It touches down
and stops to sun itself on the dock.
Wings flicker and still:
stained-glass windows
with sun shining through.

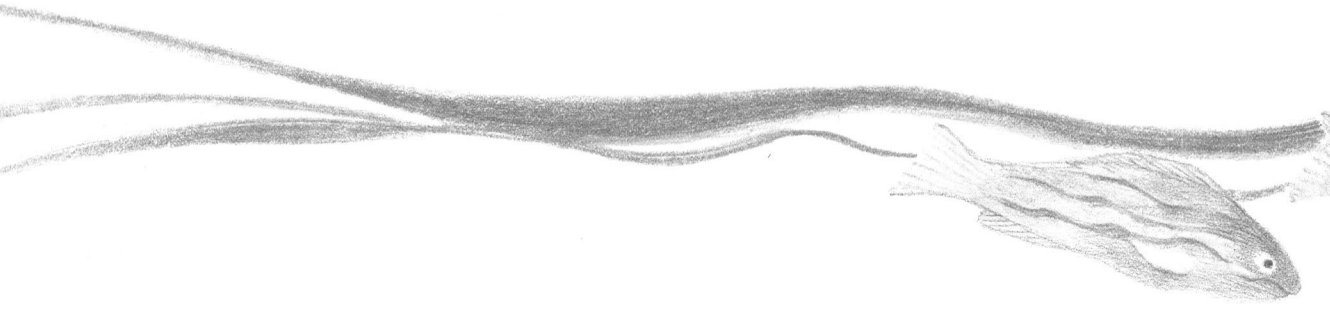

FISHES
Poem for two voices

Atlantic blue tang

        Zebra pipe

Royal gramma

        French angel

Cuban hock

        Golden butterfly

We are fishes	We are fishes
We shimmer under	We swim
	water

Our
mouths
open
and

Our
mouths

close

Our
gills
sift

air

Our
gills

from
water

Our
fins
steer
us

Our
fins

like
wings

We
are
fishes

We
are
fishes

We
shimmer

We
swim

EAGLE FLIGHT

Eagle gliding in the sky,
circling, circling way up high—
wind is whistling through your wings.
You're a graceful kite with no string.

12

DUCKS ON A WINTER NIGHT

Ducks asleep
on the banks of the pond
tuck their bills
into feathery quills,
making their own beds
to keep warm in.

MIGRATION

In the winter, we say good-bye
to the feathered compasses of the sky.

Migrating birds seldom get lost,
even with so many miles to cross.

Starlings fly by day,
using the sun to guide their way.

Warblers fly at night;
stars light up their flight.

Golden plovers are in constant motion
as they travel the Pacific Ocean.

Migrating birds don't lose their track—
when spring returns, they always come back.

WHALE CHANT

I see a
  blue whale,
  fin whale,
  humpback,
  gray,
  little piked,
  right whale,
  bottlenose,
  sei,
  killer whale,
  pilot,
  sperm, and narwhal

swimming

        in the deep

           blue sea!

THE MASKED ONE

Raccoon wears a mask
as if it's Halloween
and tiptoes through our yard
while I watch through the screen.

Clank falls the garbage-can lid to the ground,
as if raccoon is saying ''Trick or treat!''
But the cans are empty, no food to be found.
Raccoon walks away on tiny feet.

SONG OF THE DOLPHIN

I am a dolphin. I swim in the sea,
flipping and shining. Can you see me?
Now you do, and now you don't.
Try and catch me—you won't, you won't!

I jump in the air and feel so free,
twisting and turning. Can you see me?
Now you do, and now you don't.
Try and catch me—you won't, you won't!

FROG SERENADE
Poem for two voices

Ga-lunk
Ga-lunk
Ga-lunk

          I hear your

Ga-lunk

          deep-voiced songs

Ga-lunk
Ga-lunk
Ga-lunk

          by the pond

Ga-lunk

          this warm
          summer
          night.

Ga-lunk
Ga-lunk
Ga-lunk

        I hear your

Ga-lunk

        chorus of

Ga-lunk
Ga-lunk
Ga-lunk

        banjo songs

Ga-lunk

        under the shining stars
        tonight.

ELEPHANT WARNING

Walk carefully, elephants,
through the grass.
Hold out your ears
so you can hear
who may be hiding there.

Walk carefully, elephants,
through the grass.
There may be hunters
waiting to shoot you
for your long ivory tusks.

Walk carefully, elephants,
through the grass.

DRESSING LIKE A SNAKE

A snake changes its clothes
only twice a year.
Beginning with its nose,
peeling down to its toes:
new clothes suddenly appear.
Wouldn't it be nice
to dress only twice
instead of each day of the year?

24

BAT PATROL

Quickly and quietly,
the bat patrols the night,
sending an invisible song
echoing like ripples on a pond,
chasing moths around a streetlight.
Quickly and quietly,
the bat patrols the night.

THE ORB WEAVER

Weaving and weaving and weaving its web,
beginning with just a single thread—
it weaves and weaves, round and round,
until its web is strong and sound.

The spider then waits, off to one side,
and hides from insects who happen to glide
into this web of silky thread—
from which the spider soon will be fed.

FAVORITE BEAR

Grizzlies wander the meadows all day,
searching for squirrels to scamper their way.

Black bears and brown bears mark the trees,
clawing the bark, shaking the leaves.

Polar bears fish in ice and snow,
with leathery pads and fur between their toes.

Sun bear has a lighter nose than the rest
and uses its tongue to lick honey from a nest.

Although a teddy bear can't do any of these things,
it's my favorite because of all the hugs it brings.

THE GALÁPAGOS TORTOISE

The last of his kind,
one Galápagos tortoise
wanders the island for plants to eat.

The last of his kind—
sailors killed them for food,
cattle trampled their nests,
and rats ate their eggs.

The last of his kind.
Once there were thousands.
Now he's the only one.

WILL WE EVER SEE?

Will we ever see a tiger again,
stalking its prey with shining eyes?

Will we see the giant orangutan
inspecting its mate for fleas?

Or a California condor
feeding on the side of a hill?

Or a whooping crane
walking softly through a salty marsh?

Or hear the last of the blue whales
singing its sad song under the deep water?

INDEX OF TITLES AND FIRST LINES

E
H

Heard, Georgia.

Creatures of earth,
sea, and sky.

606928

$15.95

DATE